Claiborne Publications

Play and Learn

Activity Nature Book

by Chris Madsen

illustrated by Julie Hawkins and Di Eggitt

An invaluable wildlife source book with each selection of animals accompanied by two pages of activities to help children grow in their knowledge of the natural world. Knowledge is the first step to understanding and appreciating the environment around us and a beginning in the vital challenge of protection and conservation of our world.

CONTENTS

Mountain Animals

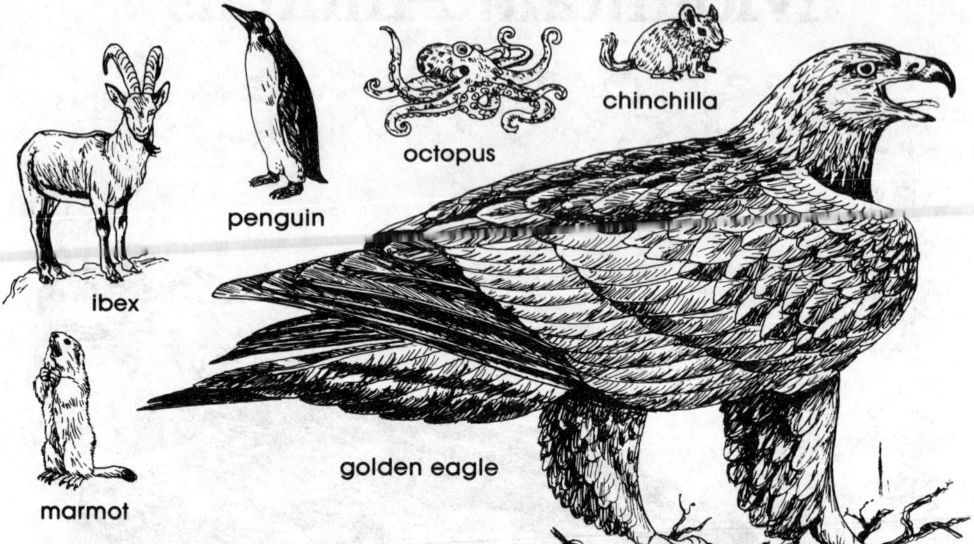

Circle the mountain animals.
Circle the animals with four legs.

I have very large horns and I am a mountain goat, circle me red.
I am like a partridge, circle me yellow.
I have fur all over my large body and hibernate in winter, circle me brown.
I am a bird of prey and have a powerful beak and claws, circle me black.
I live in a burrow in the ground and am a kind of ground squirrel, circle me blue.
I am swift like a deer and have small horns, circle me green.

Goats

Goats are a bit like sheep. The differences are in their horns—male (Billy) and female (Nanny) goats both have horns—and the funny beard that goats have.

Goats are famous for eating all sorts of peculiar things. This is because wild goats live on mountains, where there is no nice soft grass to eat. In the mountains, goats live on dry, thorny shrubs that grow in cracks in the rocks. It seems amazing that a goat's soft mouth does not get hurt by the thorns.

Another thing goats are famous for is their clever feet. Wild goats have to be mountaineers, to reach every bit of food they can see, because there is not much to eat up there. A goat's foot is very rough underneath, to grip onto rocks, and it has a marvellous sense of balance. Have you got good balance?

People have tamed goats since long ago. They are easy to feed and give us milk and meat. Wild goats still live in mountains, though. There are Rocky Mountain goats in America; mouflons in Sardinia and Corsica; ibexes in the Alps; markhors in the Himalayas.

Goats' babies are called kids. They have to be very obedient, and watch where the older goats walk and what they eat. This is how they live long enough to learn to be good mountaineers. Even though tame kids are very bouncy and may look naughty, they are just as obedient as their mountain cousins. If you get a chance to watch a kid with its mother, you will see it walks exactly where she walks, stops when she stops, and nibbles what she nibbles.

Migrating Birds

Circle the birds that are here for the winter.
Circle the birds that go away for the winter.

I lay eggs in other birds' nests, circle me yellow.
I have a long neck and snowy feathers, circle me blue.
I feed on insects and save them for later on prickly branches, circle me green.
I have a very long forked tail, circle me orange.
I have a white rump and a short forked tail, circle me red.
I fly to Europe in the winter. Don't mistake me for a very large duck! Circle me brown.

Migrating Birds

Some birds that nest in Britain in the summer find it too cold in winter, so they fly away south towards Africa. We say goodbye to swallows, swifts and martins when the autumn comes, and to many little warblers, too.

But at the same time as these birds are leaving us, some others are arriving. These are birds that nest in the far North, in the Arctic Circle. They also fly southwards for the winter, but Britain and Canada are quite warm enough to please them.

Swallows leave Great Britain in winter to fly to Africa.

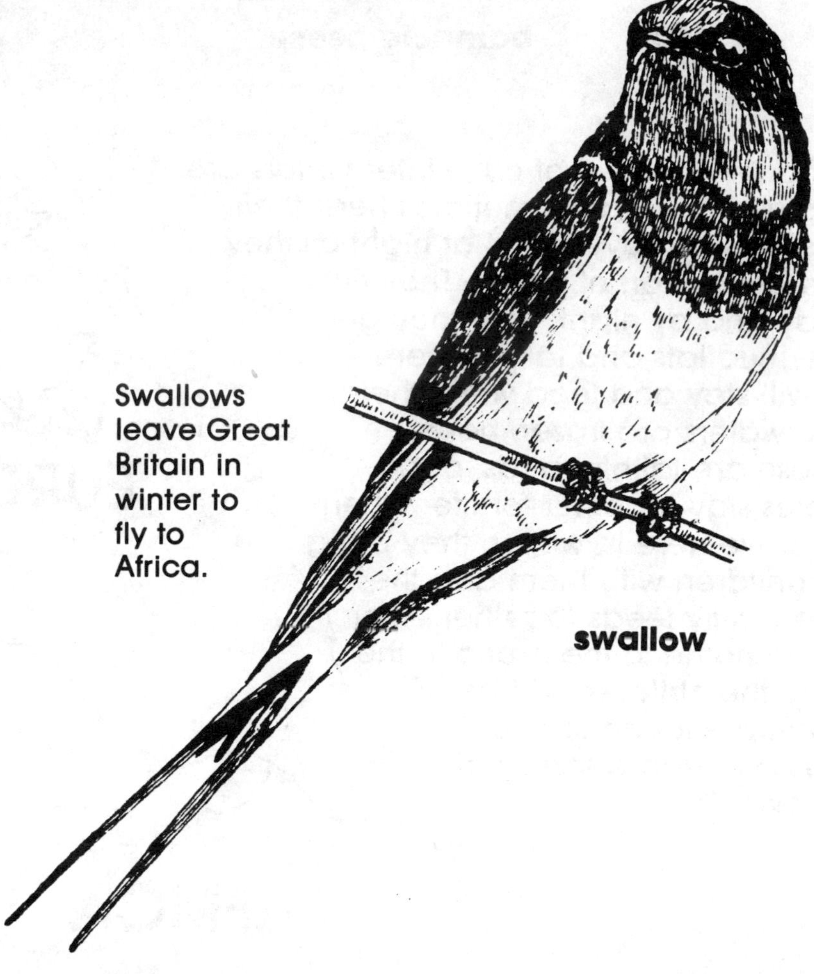

swallow

In winter
geese come
from the
Arctic to
Great Britain.

barnacle geese

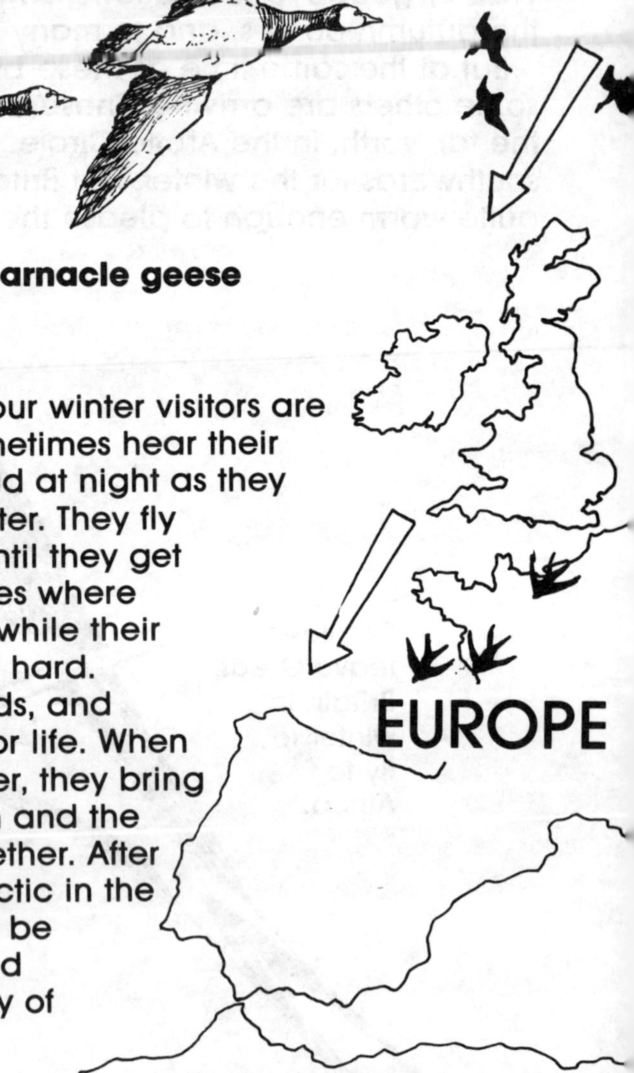

Among the loveliest of our winter visitors are the geese. You can sometimes hear their wings whistling overhead at night as they arrive at the start of winter. They fly by day and by night, until they get to the mudflats and lakes where they will stay and feed while their Arctic waters are frozen hard.

Geese are faithful birds, and couples stay together for life. When they arrive here in winter, they bring their children with them and the whole family feeds together. After they go home to the Arctic in the spring, the children will be grown-up enough to find mates and start a family of their own.

Baby Animals

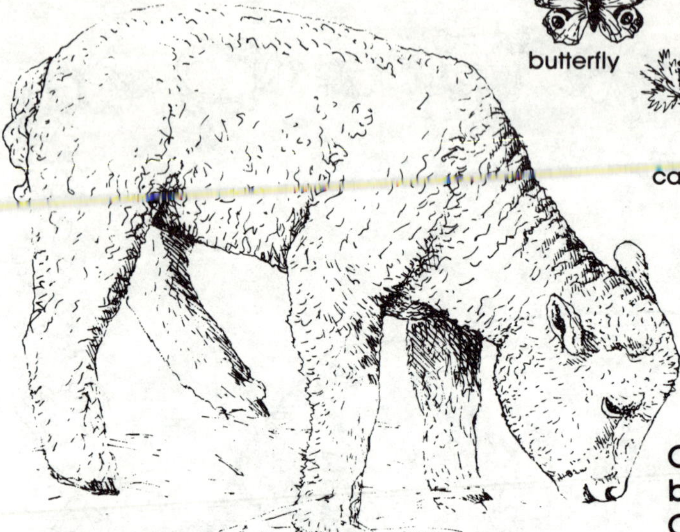

lamb

butterfly

chick

caterpillar

piglet

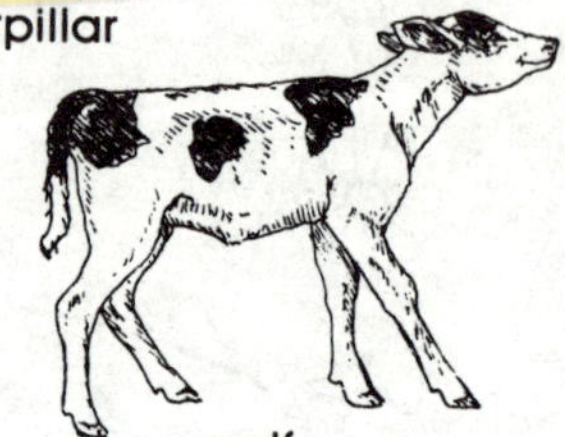

calf

Circle in red the baby animals.
Circle in blue the animals with four legs.

caterpillar

puppy

tadpole

lamb

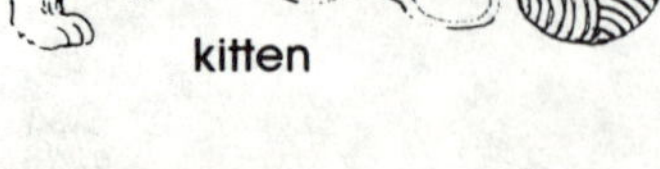

kitten

chick

I grow up to be a dog, circle me red.
I grow up to be a chicken, circle me yellow.
I grow up to be a butterfly, circle me blue.
I grow up to be a sheep, circle me brown.
I grow up to be a frog, circle me black.
I grow up to be a cat, circle me green.

Chicks

Little fluffy chicks are chickens' babies. They grow inside an egg laid by their mother, while she sits on the egg to keep it warm. Not all eggs will grow chicks, though. Most of the eggs you have for your breakfast haven't got a chick inside at all because they were not fertilised. This means the hen who laid the egg did not mate with a cockerel.

When a chick is ready to hatch out of its egg, it has to break the eggshell from inside. There is a little bump at the end of its beak, and it uses this bump to chip a hole in the eggshell.

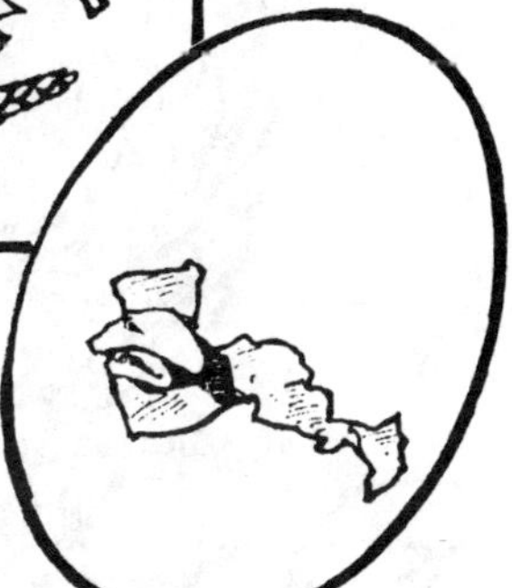

Chicks are ready to look around them for food just as soon as they are hatched. They peck at anything they see, and their mother helps them to learn what is good to eat. She helps her chicks to learn about danger, too, and cuddles them under her wings to keep them warm at night.

The little chicks grow up very quickly. In a little while, they are covered with feathers and ready to leave their mother. Some will be hens and some will be cockerels.

Molluscs

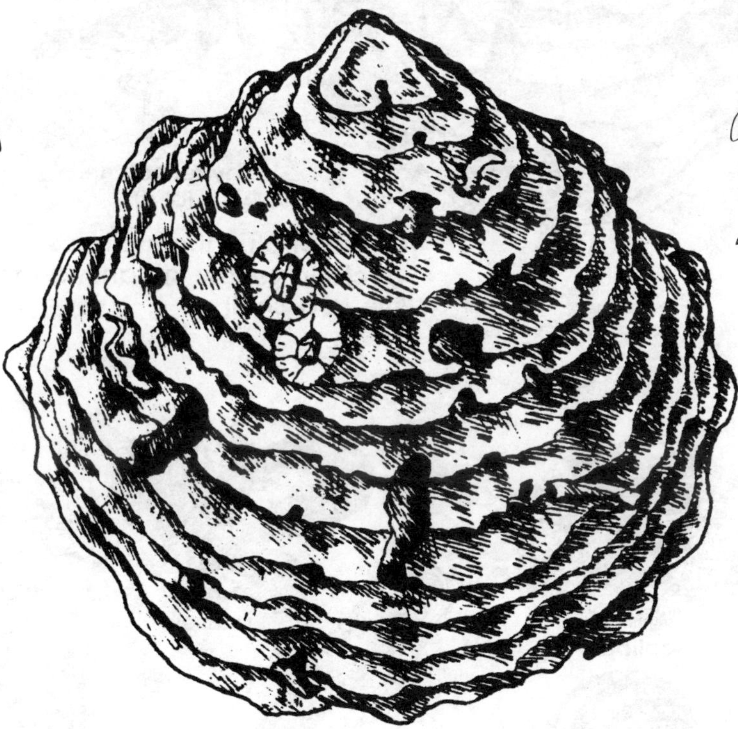

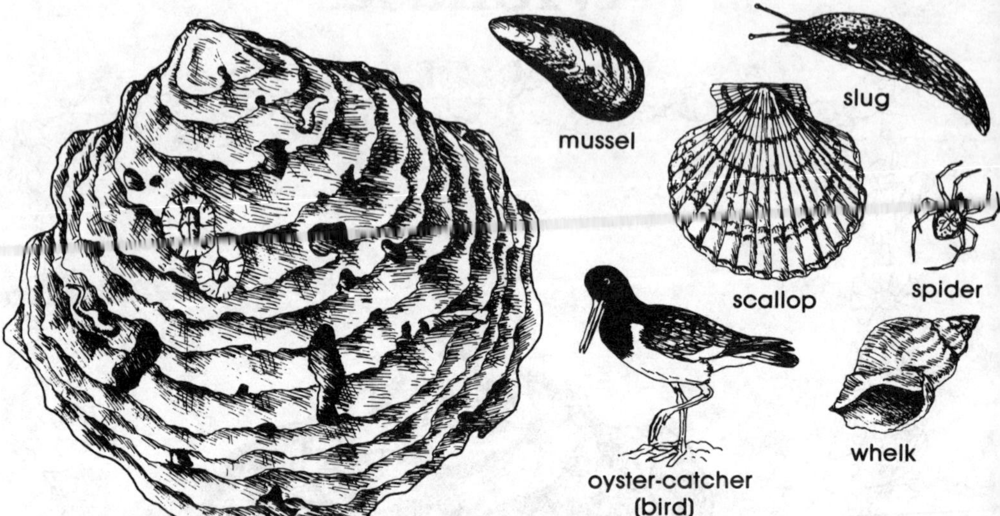

Circle in blue the molluscs.
Circle in yellow the animals that live in a shell.

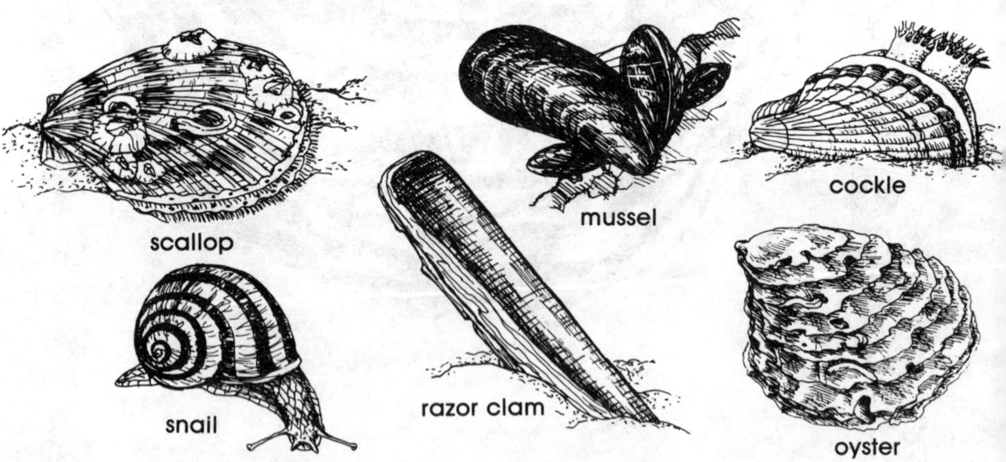

I am a long, thin mollusc that burrows into the sand, circle me red.
We are black-shelled molluscs that live in groups on rocks, circle us blue.
I have two small horns and a striped curly shell, circle me brown.
My shell is layered like a ruffled skirt and I make pearls, circle me green.
I live partly buried in sand and have siphons to catch passing food, circle me orange
My shell is fluted and I am often covered with barnacles, circle me yellow.

Oysters

Oysters are molluscs, relations of cockles, mussels and clams. They have two shells— and they live in the sea.

Baby oysters (larvae) are very, very small. They swim about in the sea for a week or two until they find somewhere nice to settle down. Then they lie down on their left side and glue themselves firmly to the rock.

mussel

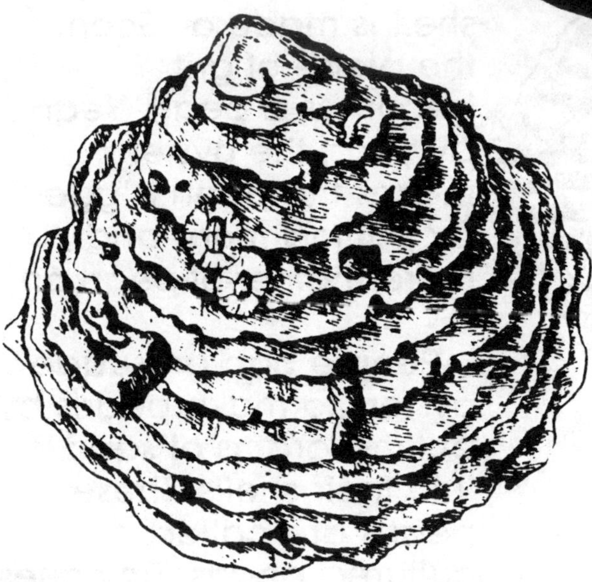

oyster

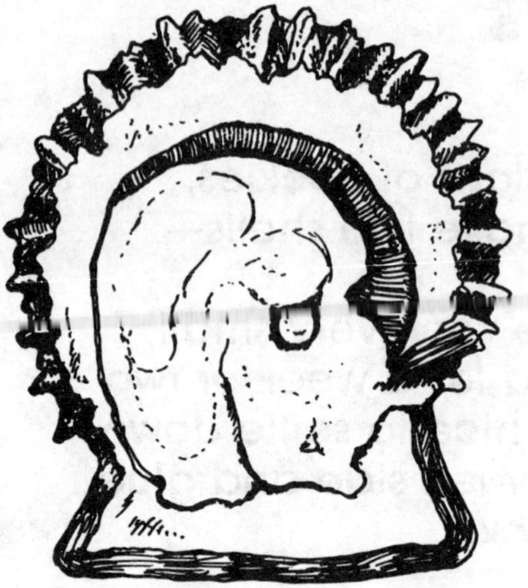

oyster and pearl

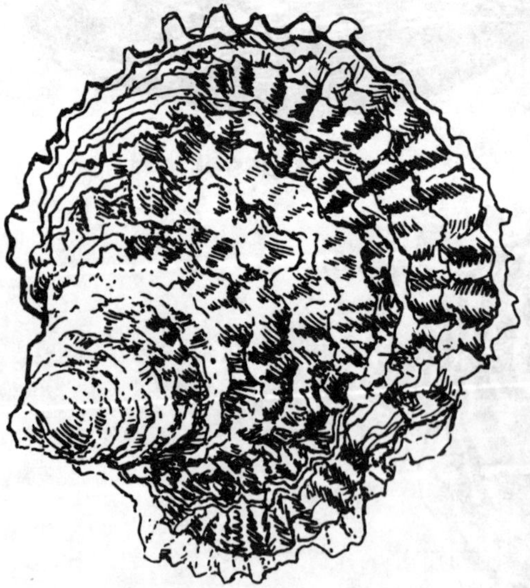

great American pearl oyster

Lying on the sea bed, oysters suck in water and strain out tiny plants to eat. They can only live in very clean seas.

The outside of an oyster shell is rough and lumpy, but the inside is smooth and very pretty. When a bit of sand or grit gets into an oyster's shell, it feels rough and uncomfortable. The oyster makes it more comfortable by covering the grit with a smooth coat of the same stuff its shell is made of. Soon, the piece of grit becomes a pearl. Year by year, the oyster makes the pearl bigger by putting more and more mother-of-pearl on it.

People can persuade oysters to make pearls by putting grains of sand into their shells. These pearls are called cultured pearls. Tiny ones are called seed pearls.

Owls

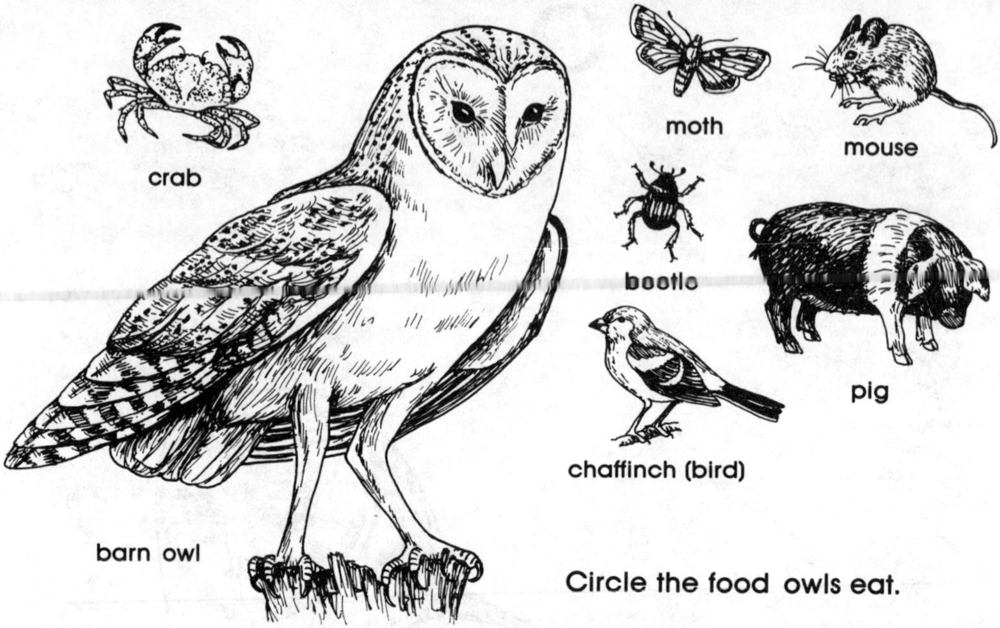

Circle the food owls eat.

I have a white heart-shaped face and I like nesting in barns. Circle me red.

I am a large white owl with feathery legs and I eat lemmings and voles. Circle me yellow.

I have long ear-tufts and a long body and my food includes rats and mice. Circle me green.

I am a tiny owl. I live a the cactus plant and eat beetles and moths. Circle me blue.

I have a rounded head and large eyes. I roost in trees and eat rodents, birds and insects. Circle me purple.

I have long legs and live in abandoned burrows. Circle me brown.

Owls

Owls are night birds. The farmer calls barn owls flying cats because they help keep his barn clear of rats and mice.

barn owl

Barn owls really do like barns. They nest in hollow trees, too. You can see barn owls flying along ditches in twilight, at dusk and dawn, floating silently on pale wings.

Tawny owls are hardly ever seen. They generally wait until it is really dark before coming out to hunt. Tawny owls are the ones that go 'to-whit-to-woo', though, so they are often heard. Barn owls are also called screech owls, which tells you what they say.

Owls are clever hunters. Their huge eyes can use a kind of light our eyes can't see (called infra-red), which helps them to pick out tiny mice and even beetles scurrying on the ground. They have big ears, too, and can hear a pine needle move.

Owl babies have to spend a long time learning to hunt before they can go and look after themselves. Owls hatched in the spring don't leave their parents until late autumn, and their parents have to feed them for nearly four months.

Owls eat mice, birds, beetles, and even moths when food is scarce. They swallow their prey whole, and have a special way of coughing up the skin and bones they cannot digest. The bones and skin are wrapped up in a pellet, which may be found on the ground under an owl's favourite perch. Different kinds of owls make different shaped pellets.

Grass Eating Animals

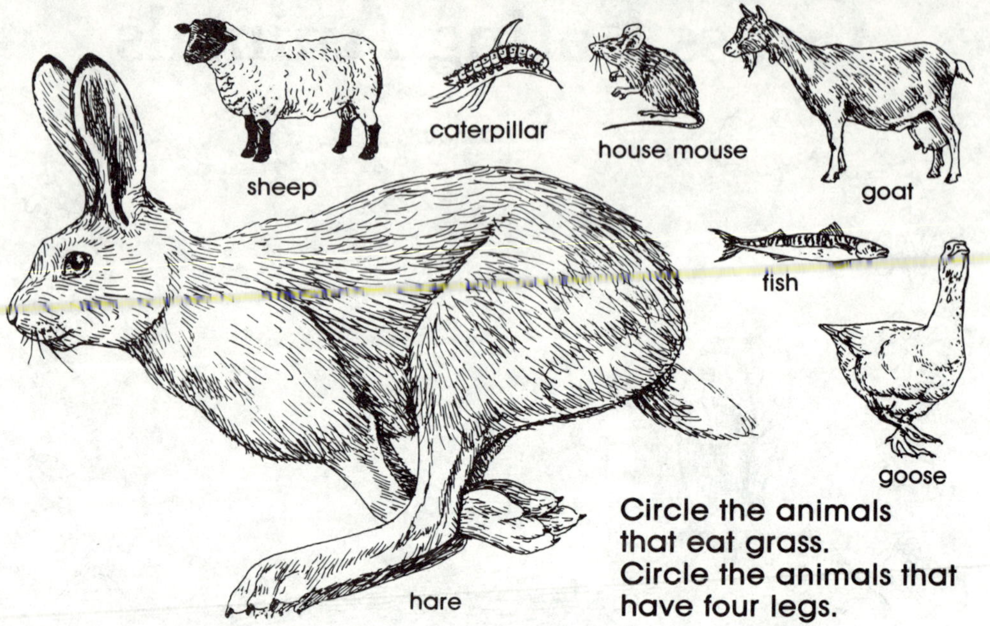

Circle the animals that eat grass.
Circle the animals that have four legs.

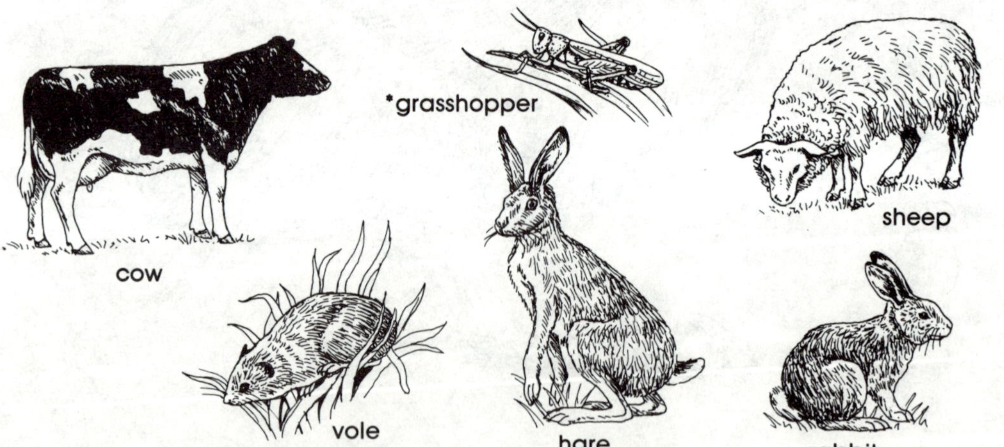

I have a woolly coat and eat grass: circle me green.
I am an insect and very good at hopping among the grass blades: circle me yellow.
I have long ears with black tips and a slender, alert body: circle me blue.
I give milk which humans drink, and am a large grass-eater: circle me orange.
I look like a mouse but have a shorter tail: circle me brown.
I too have long ears, but not as long as my relation the hare's: circle me red.

Hares

Hares are relations of rabbits but, although they eat the same sort of green things, they are quite different. Rabbits like to live in big families; hares live alone. Rabbits dig holes; hares don't dig at all.

If you look carefully at a hare, you will see it has very long black-tipped ears. It also has very long, strong back legs, and can run very fast. A hare's eyes are a beautiful gold colour.
In the spring, hares seem to go mad. Instead of being shy, they go jumping about in all the places where they live. You can see hares having boxing matches in the spring, standing up high on their back legs and fighting. Sometimes, two males (bucks) may be fighting for a mate.

Sometimes the fight is between a female hare (doe) and a buck she doesn't want for a mate.

A mother hare makes a nest in the grass (called a form) to have her babies (leverets). She leaves the little helpless leverets there while she goes out to feed herself, and only comes back to give them milk. After a few days, she moves each leveret to a separate form. This means that if a fox finds one of them the others are still safe. Leverets keep very still and are very hard to see. When they are grown up, they will be able to run at 35 mph for as much as 4 miles without getting tired!

Bats

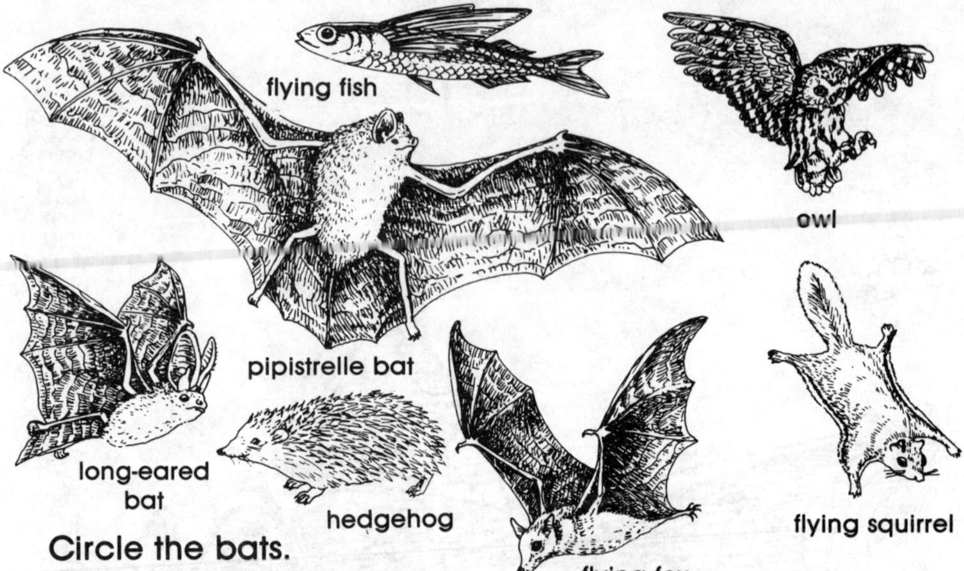

Circle the bats.
Circle the flying animals

I have long ears and am a bat, circle me brown.
I have a fox shaped face, circle me yellow.
I am not a bat and have a long black tipped tail, circle me black.
I am the smallest bat, circle me red.
I have a horseshoe shaped nose, circle me blue.
I am not a bat and have a furry body, circle me orange.

Bats

Bats are the only furry animals that can really, truly fly. Their hands have turned into wings, by growing very long fingers that have a web of thin skin joining them together.

A lot of birds eat insects that fly in the daytime. Bats take over at dusk, and many of them eat the night-flying insects, like moths.

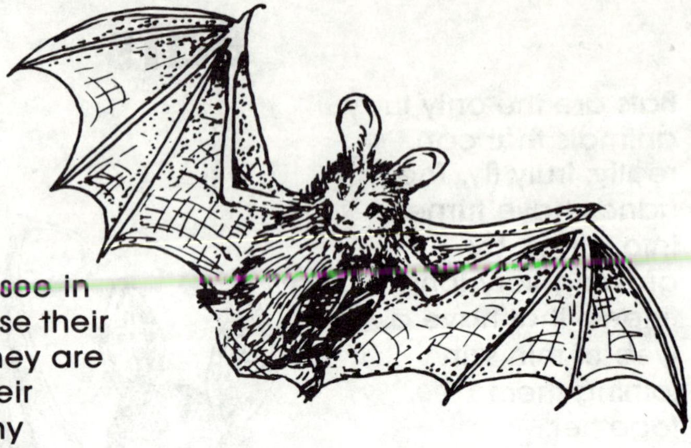

Because it is hard to see in the dark, most bats use their ears to 'see' where they are going, and to find their food. A bat makes tiny squeaks as it flies, and these squeaks bounce off things in front of it. The bat's wonderful ears can hear the echo of its squeak and tell exactly what the squeak has bounced off, and exactly where it is.

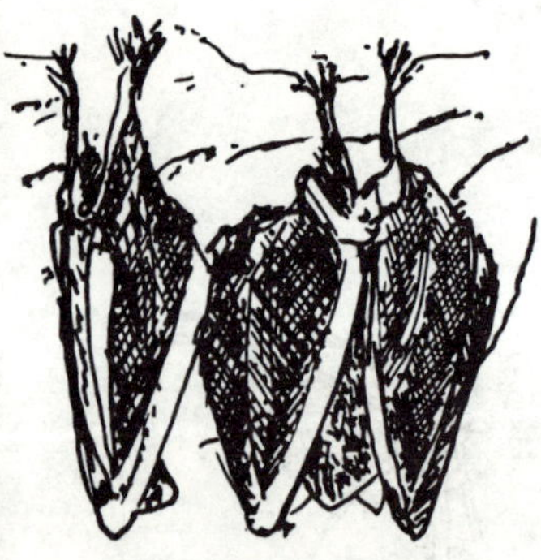

Bats have their babies in a special place called a 'nursery'. The babies are never left alone; some of the mothers take it in turn to stay with them while others go out to eat. When the babies get older, they go out with their mother, clinging to her fur while she flies about.

There are many silly stories about bats, and here are three of the silliest:

BATS DO NOT GET TANGLED IN YOUR HAIR. They are clever enough to spot a gnat in the dark, remember.

BATS ARE NOT DIRTY OR SMELLY. If bats live in your roof, it must be clean—they don't like dirty places.

BATS ARE NOT BLIND. They all have bright little eyes—and fruit bats have really big eyes.

Arachnids

Spiders

Have you ever found a spider in your bath? If you have, it was probably a house spider that fell in by mistake and couldn't climb out again. These spiders do not make pretty webs. Their web is an untidy tangle, but makes a good fly-trap. Your mother probably knows it is a good dust-trap too!

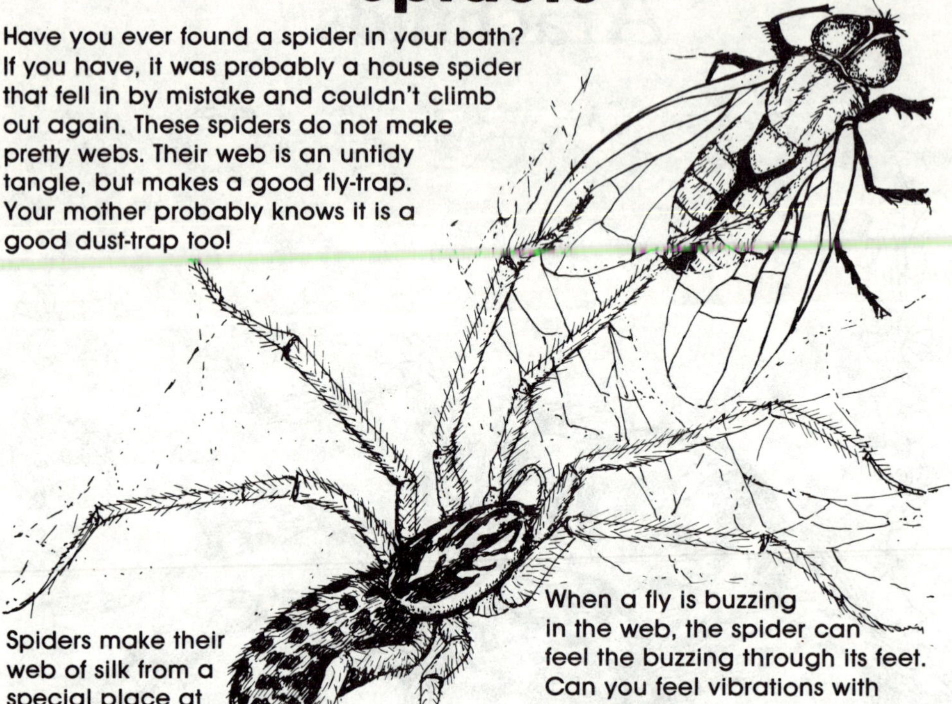

Spiders make their web of silk from a special place at the back of their body. They use their back legs to guide the thread. How many legs do spiders have?

When a fly is buzzing in the web, the spider can feel the buzzing through its feet. Can you feel vibrations with your fingers?

It runs across the web and bites the fly, then eats it, leaving an empty shell. Having spiders in your house is a good way not to have flies!

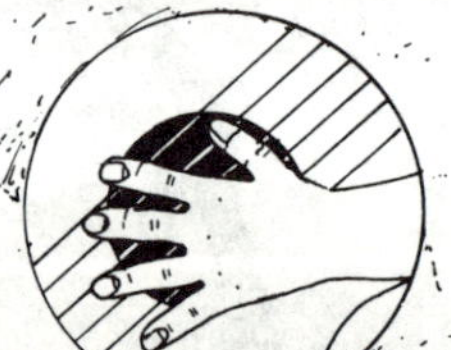

A female spider lays her eggs in a bundle of silk called a cocoon. She guards the cocoon until her babies hatch. They are very tiny.

You can keep a house spider in a fish-tank. It will make a web there, and all you have to do is give it a live fly sometimes. Some people don't like spiders. The ones in Britain are not dangerous to people, only to flies. You're not afraid of spiders, are you?